A Letter to Trump Supporters

Unleash Your Power

Kevin M. Fahrner

ISBN: 978-1-312-15066-9

Table of Contents

Dear Trump Supporters,

I hope you are doing well.

I am writing you this letter to share some books and articles I have read about the state of the country we both live in and love, and I welcome your feedback. First, I'd like to say—as a fellow American—I, too, want our country to improve. I want the economy to thrive, for people to be kinder to each other, for us to be able to look after our families and live our lives prosperously in this great country.

Like you most likely are, I am concerned about the division in the country and the lack of leadership in Washington. I am tired of the drama. The finger-pointing. The name-calling. Our politicians use all the tools of manipulation for votes and division to keep themselves in power.

I remember when I was introduced to the phrase *performance politics*. This is where a politician hosts an event or delivers a speech to create a specific emotion in the audience without providing solutions or truly addressing the seriousness of any issue. The politician who practices performance politics is looking for fame and fortune.

Sometimes, these messages are hopeful, positively inspiring, and can fill our hearts with love. However, performance politics is almost always intended to confuse and instill the primal emotions of fear and rage in us. When giving these sorts of speeches, many leaders attempt to "externalize" our grievances and create invisible enemies so we get worked up over people who may be our neighbors or different than us instead of focusing on the leaders and our country's politics.

Aren't you exhausted with the political discourse? Are you being whipped up into a passionate frenzy about various issues, making you feel negatively toward your fellow American citizens and the others who have moved to this fine country to create a better life for themselves and their families? Whatever happened to draining the swamp?

You, me, and everyone else in this country have some unfinished business to attend to.

As a lifelong and passionate observer of American politics, I have come to the conclusion that the Trump coalition is the only block of voters who can turn Washington around in one or two election cycles. You have a significant amount of power within the American project. I hope you understand the power you have and use it wisely. The two leading political parties—Democrats and Republicans—and leading media companies like CNN and Fox News are afraid of you. Congressmen and senators are afraid to speak the truth because they fear being voted out of office. Fox News ratings go down when they say anything considered unsupportive of Trump.

David Bauder and the *Associated Press* reported on February 18, 2023, the following:

According to the Nielsen Company, Fox News tumbled from first to third in the news network ratings between the November 3, 2020, election and Biden's inauguration on Jan. 20, 2021. Meanwhile, thousands of Fox viewers flocked to the more conservative Newsmax, where prime-time viewership shot from 58,000 the week before the election to 568,000 the week after.

This behavior is not good for the country. We need to reward the truth and be able to change our opinion(s) if the facts change. If we do not support the truth, then the foundation of this country will shift and crumble beneath us as if made of sand. To make a great nation, we need a strong foundation. Doing this means supporting the truth even if it causes us pain. There is no shame in changing your position when you are presented with different information. *The goal is to improve our country,* not to be correct all the time.

There's a distinction between Trump and The Trump Coalition. The coalition is much more important to American politics and will last longer than Trump. It will require work to defend against misinformation and support the truth. However, as the Trump Coalition joins other groups who put the country first, the progress we can achieve will be rapid and will improve the lives of many Americans and build a strong America.

Trump is powerless without you. All of his power comes from you. If you move your support to another candidate, the power moves with it.

Unfortunately, due to the fear many have about your power, Congress, senators, and the media have concluded their survival is contingent on feeding you lies. The problem is these media companies and politicians weaponize your outrage and use it to improve their ratings and contribute to the primal fear the politicians want you to be in. When we are in fear or angry states of mind, we seek certainty and want to take action against what it is we are afraid or angry toward. We must be careful to understand why a message is being passed to us. We must then ask the following essential question: Is the fear I feel valid, or am I being manipulated? I want to know why you feel anger or fear. I want to hear about the important issues giving you concerns about our country.

First, I want you to understand that you, the Trump coalition, have a choice. You can help us make the next twenty four years pleasant or continue the drama we are currently seeing in Washington. The great power you have comes with great responsibility. The election of 2024 could be as significant as 1995 or 2000. In 1995, the Republicans took the House for the first time in fifty-eight years. In 2000, when George W. Bush and Al Gore, two opposing candidates, vied for the presidency, the courts deemed Bush president due to a close race in Florida.

The election of 2024 has the chance to get Washington and the country back on track. We need the Trump coalition to lead the way.

So please, dear Trump supporter, read this letter with an open mind. I'm only here to have a dialogue with you, and I want to know what you think in return. At the end of this book is my email address. I welcome your thoughts, concerns, and insights.

Chapter One

CORRUPTION

What are we trying to fix?

I think about politics every day of my life and have been following it for all of my adult years. How to solve our country's issues dominates my head daily, as does research, conversation, and solutions-oriented thinking regarding our political and social issues. I imagine a musician hears music in his or her head most of the day—and that's what it's like for me. It just so happens that what I hear is politics.

It started in high school. It amazed me that World War II had only ended fifteen years before I was born, and I would research and try to imagine what life would have been like for everyone in the world during that time. It was hard for me to imagine that such a horrible series of events had taken place shortly before my lifetime.

My interest in politics continued as a young adult. I watched and followed a series of bad outcomes resulting from bad decisions. Here are a few examples of preventable decisions once we elect the right type of representatives:

- The Savings and Loan Bank crisis in the late 1980s, when the US government lost $500 billion
- The 2001 Bush tax cut created a deficit for the federal government. According to a March 2023 *Washington Post* article by Jeff Stein, the Bush tax cuts were responsible for $1.5 trillion of our national debt.
- The invasion of Iraq cost the American people $3 trillion—of which over one million people were reported to have died.
- The 2008 financial crisis. This financial crisis had a devastating impact on most Americans and negatively impacted our standing in the world.
- 1980 to the present, where American jobs were outsourced to low-cost regions without oversight.

The winners in the above events are the highest wage earners and large corporations and politicians. The biggest losers? We, the American people, and our children and grandchildren.

Where did the $3 trillion we spent on the Iraq war go? To give an idea of how much money that really is, It breaks down to $30,000 for 100 million households. We must work together to ensure our leaders do not repeat this mistake.

On September 11, 2021, Linda J. Bilmes summarized in detail the recipients of the trillions spent on the war. Reading the article was deeply informative to understand how wasteful we are with our money. Here are two key highlights from the article:

1. No matter how much Washington bickers about what has been achieved in the spending of $3tn on "forever wars," the only standout winner is the US defense industry.

2. Since 2001, the defense sector has spent $2.4 billion lobbying Congress, even directly contributing to campaigns for most members of Congress.

A Better Response to 9/11

On September 11, 2001, two planes crashed into the World Trade Center Twin Towers in New York. What George Bush should have said a month or two after 9/11—rather than starting an unjust war—is the following:

> *The 9/11 attack was conducted by fifty-five individuals. We know where they're located, and we know their names. It does not make any sense to send in a million-man army to bring fifty-five people to justice. We will bring them to justice in our time frame, when it's convenient to us using all the powers of our intelligence agencies and our military to strategically bring these people to justice. In the meantime, let's continue to pray for the 2,977 victims and their families.*

Some would say this is Monday morning quarterbacking, but I, and many others, could have written this in December of 2001. The voices for peace were drowned out by the voices of war—headed by the military industry. It was

4

obvious to anyone paying attention that Iraq had no role in 9/11.

Morality in Leaders and Corporations

Many of our leaders lack the moral fiber necessary to govern, lead, and influence. Both government and businesses lack the essential morality needed to drive our country forward. Morality is not represented anywhere and does not have a voice at the table where decisions are made. Instead, profit and "progress" dominate. Although profit is essential to a company, blindly increasing the numbers without worrying about how it affects humans, animals, and the planet shows our focus to be in the wrong place.

In short, when executives at our large corporations make decisions, morality is absent. Let's look at these examples of corporations ignoring the morality of their decisions.

Facebook/Meta

In an October 5, 2021, article by *NPR*, writer Bobby Allyn summarizes the testimony of data scientist Frances Haugen, a former employee at Facebook. In her testimony, she stated, "Facebook harms children, sows division and undermines democracy in pursuit of breakneck growth and astronomical profits."

Haugen leaked one Facebook study finding that 13.5 percent of UK teen girls in one survey stated their suicidal thoughts became "more frequent" after they started using Instagram (which is owned by Facebook). Another leaked study found that 17 percent of teen girls experienced a worsening of their eating disorders after using Instagram. Also, about 32 percent of teen girls said that when they felt bad about their bodies, Instagram made them feel worse. Haugen told Congress outside researchers and lawmakers had asked how Facebook affected the health and safety of children, and the company didn't give answers.

The above is clear evidence Facebook chooses to mislead and demands of us to believe they are a force for good in the world. Haugen also reported to Congress that the algorithms reward engagement. In other words, if I post something and it receives interactions, such as "likes" or "comments," it spreads more widely and is more likely to feature more prominently in feeds, as opposed to the feed showing posts chronologically. This helps boost sensationalized content, especially on posts featuring rage, hate, and fear—and this, according to Haugen, helps misinformation travel far and wide.

In my mind, Facebook executives and middle managers sit around the conference table looking at the numbers, understanding the harm and manipulation generated, and instead of pulling back, they choose to put the pedal to the metal and keep expanding at the expense of the health of adults, nations, and—crucially—our children.

Wells Fargo

Wells Fargo settled with the Justice Department in 2012 for their involvement in the subprime mortgage scandal. The Justice Department found Wells Fargo "steered" customers into subprime loans where they paid higher fees and risked defaulting on the loan once the artificial interest rate expired and the loan adjusted to market rate.

In 2020, Wells Fargo was forced to pay $3 billion for creating "fake" accounts. Wells Fargo employees created millions of savings and checking accounts for customers without their knowledge or approval.

In 2021, Wells Fargo paid $72 million to settle the Justice Department's lawsuit after the agency found the bank overcharged hundreds of currency exchange customers.

In December 2022, according to a *Nerdwallet* article written by Cara Smith on April 25, 2023, the Consumer Financial Protection Bureau ordered Wells Fargo to pay $1.7 billion in fines and $2 billion in consumer redress in connection with "illegal activity" across several of its product lines.

Purdue Pharma

Purdue Pharma played a significant role in the opioid crisis and paid a $6 billion fine. The opioid crisis was responsible for thirteen million Americans becoming addicted to opioids and 300,000 deaths as a result of using OxyContin. The book *DreamLand* by Sam Quinones covers this topic in detail.

PGA vs. LIV Golf

At some point in 2021, the LIV tour offered very large sums of money to elite golfers to play in their league. The money ranged from tens of millions to hundreds of millions. The criteria were simple—all the players had to do was play, and it didn't matter if they won or not, as the money was guaranteed. Initially, there was some outrage against the players who went to the new league as the league is financed by Saudi Arabia, whose human rights record and treatment of women is—at the very least—suspect.

The players who refused to play for the new league passed on anywhere from $25 million to $100 million. I commend those with the moral code to say no to the money. However, I don't blame or fault the players who went to the new league. They were offered sums of money that would set them and their families up for generations. They make these choices without having good role models to look up to. How many in society are choosing the moral solution? Not many.

In June 2023, sadly, the PGA sold the league to the Saudi league. It is too early to understand why, but there was no way the PGA could compete financially with oil money from Saudi Arabia. However, there were many lawsuits filed against PGA, and I speculate these could have put the PGA into bankruptcy.

The above examples show three things; One, money has an overwhelming influence on our society. Two, some people will do horrible things to obtain money. Three, morality does not have enough influence on decision-making.

Unfortunately, the loss of morality in our government, companies, and institutions is the root cause of the decline in the standard of living of the average American and the United States' position as a global role model.

In order to restore morality in our corporations, we first need to restore it in our government.

The Game Is Played by the Rules Congress Makes

In 1938, Congress passed the Fair Labor Standards Act, which required all employers to pay overtime for any worker who worked more than forty-four hours a week. Two years later, the number of hours was reduced to forty. From then on, the forty-hour work week was established alongside the creation of the weekend. I can almost hear the outcry from business leaders against the legislation. But they all survived.

That is the way the system is designed to work. Congress makes the rules, and corporations follow. However, we face a different reality today. Big corporations write the legislation. Let's look at how a company functions versus our government.

A company builds a product and sells the product to customers. A typical practice is getting customer feedback on the product, and the company uses this feedback to improve the product. This creates a helpful feedback loop between the company and the customer and can improve the product, which helps the company sell a better product (making capital) and keeps the customer happy (with an improved product). Contrast this to the political world.

Three groups of people are involved in an election: the candidate, the group funding the candidate (donors), and the citizens who have to live with the legislation, either passed or not passed. Unfortunately, the donors fund the candidate's election, and once the candidate wins, the donors either *help* or *completely write* the legislation. I want to reiterate the donors—who are self-interested—get to write laws favorable to them in terms of money and power. This process is little more than bribery; if large corporations offer their financial muscle to help a campaign, they are going to demand something in return.

As we've all seen, these large corporations act corruptly. Would you want big pharma, oil, or social media companies knowingly harming children to write your laws? The candidates are in the pockets of corporations; rarely do they ask the citizens what they want. They just rely on them for votes. This is why we have a swamp; our best interests are not respected. Legislation is written by donors and corporations who are only looking out for themselves. It is you and me, and our fellow citizens, who suffer.

In an article published by the *Brennan Center for Justice* dated December 12, 2019, Tim Lau wrote the following:

January 21, 2020, will mark a decade since the Supreme Court's ruling in *Citizens United v. Federal Election Commission*, a controversial decision that reversed century-old campaign finance restrictions and enabled corporations and other outside groups to spend unlimited funds on elections.

This ruling, referred to as Citizens United, concluded corporations are people, and money is speech. Does this ruling make any sense to you?

Since this was a Supreme Court ruling, the only way to drain the swamp in this instance is to pass an amendment. So I propose a new amendment: The Election Integrity Act of 2024.

The Election Integrity Act of 2024 states corporations are not people as it pertains in part or whole to elections and campaign contributions. This covers the entire campaigning and election process. Money is not considered speech as it pertains to campaigns and elections. Money can be regulated when it comes to campaign financing. All elections in every state for the Senate and the House will use Rank Choice Voting. Gerrymandering is illegal; districts will be created by longitude and latitude.

In short, if you are serious about draining the swamp, you must support legislation similar to what I proposed above to get money out of the process.

How We Vote

As we discussed briefly, our politicians and leading media outlets today spend most of their time trying to get us to be emotional, as we'll more likely tune in, increasing their ratings, which in turn ups their income. They instill fear in us to put us in panic mode, to keep us gripped by the slanted drama they are selling to us. Once we are in panic mode, thought and reason do not participate in our decision-making process. Instead, we are ruled by carefully manipulated emotions.

Being Intellectually Curious in the Complex World

Many Americans are taught not to be intellectually curious and to trust the elders, church leaders, or others who occupy a position of authority without their input. They are taught this from a young age, and this is ingrained into their behavioral patterns.

I would suggest to anyone who sees themselves in the above statement to question this philosophy. Our democracy is dependent on each and every citizen to be informed about the issues pertaining to it. One of the unique characteristics of humans is our ability to reason. But we must educate ourselves and find our own reason, not just follow another's without question.

The internet has made researching easier than ever. The only warning I would give is to be aware of the source of the information. Does the source's author have an economic interest in what they promote? Are they well-cited when giving facts? Are they trying to weaponize your outrage or inform you? Are they open to your feedback or dictating to you?

Our world is increasing in complexity, the growing problem with misinformation, the development of deep fakes, and the proliferating sophistication of AI. The only way for us to protect ourselves individually and as a nation is for each citizen to be vigilant in finding the truth.

In 1980, I supported Reagan. However, by the end of his term, I found myself unable to defend his policies. I realized I didn't have enough information, and I couldn't just trust my thoughts—often based on emotional reactions—without additional research.

When reading an article or book or listening to a speech, I look for words trying to elicit emotion. This is a red flag for me. Name-calling—Marxist, liberal, socialist, fascist, RINO—are often words used out of context to trigger (often negative) emotional reactions. Do not let your sources manipulate you with trigger words.

Emotions

The *Merriam-Webster Dictionary* defines "emotion" as: "A conscious mental reaction. Subjectively experienced as strong feelings usually directed toward a specific object and typically accompanied by behavioral changes in the body."

I find this definition compelling. For me, the keyword is "reaction," as it is an action taken in direct response to something. It conveys a loss of control—like when we are "reactive" to a political speech. I also find the word "subjectively" in this context informative. According to Merriam-Webster, "subjective" is "characteristic of or belonging to reality as perceived rather as independent of the mind." The important word there is "perceived." The dictionary also states the opposite of subjective is "objective." The definition of objective is "expressing or dealing with facts or conditions as perceived without distortion by personal feelings, prejudices or interpretations."

So what's most important? Subjective interpretation or objective interpretation? In essence, both are important, even though one (subjective) is more likely to give an unfair slanting. Subjectivity isn't all bad, though. We often think of our kids as the most precious humans in the world—a subjective interpretation, as another father or mother would say about their own kids. But when it comes to the facts of the matter, let's say a corporation's illegal or immoral dealings, objective measures of corruption are more likely to be helpful.

Of course, emotions will always play a role in our decision-making and thinking. But we need to balance it with good information from multiple sources.

Let's explore a personal anecdote.

I am a Raider football fan. To me, they are the most important football team in the world. This is a subjective statement. If we were to go on most Super Bowl wins, the most important (or successful) football team is the New England Patriots. This is an objective (though metric-dependent) measure of importance.

My brother and my two boys are also Raiders fans. When we watch a Raider game, everything is emotion—we lose touch with our rational functions. We react emotionally to the events of the game, and we lose control of our behavior when we score a touchdown—jumping around the living room and hugging. However, we recognize how irrational our behavior is, but we spend little to no time trying to control it.

When I watch TV and look at the crowds, I realize I am not alone in my behavior when it comes to fans of sports teams. One time, I watched the Warriors play the Lakers in the NBA playoffs. I watched with a Lakers fan, which is rare because when we watch football, we watch alone and make sure only Raider fans are in the house—we don't want someone else rooting the other way for fear of clashing! During the basketball game, the Lakers made shots, the Warriors missed shots, and the officiating kept going in favor of the Lakers. I couldn't control my emotions or outbursts, even though I watched in mixed company, and the Warriors don't mean that much to me.

As someone born and raised in Northern California, I, like many others, learned at an early age to hate the Lakers (and the Dodgers, but that's a story for another time). This prejudice against other sports teams is conveyed early and reinforced with every game they play against each other.

It's completely nonsensical. A kid is brainwashed to support one team over the other. Now, let's look at an extra level of absurdity—this brainwashed thinking also happens with politics, where it makes even less sense. Should we really be treating our support of political parties like sports teams?

Think about it; as a kid, you don't know why you hate the Dodgers (or any other team). You just do. You will attempt to rationalize this hatred to yourself after your emotional outburst, like how people get when they hear "Republicans" or "Democrats." The world of politics isn't about point scoring, although our leaders will lead us to believe that, so we continue to vote for and support them.

Letting your emotions flow during a sporting event is appropriate, as long as you don't spill over into overt violence or act harmfully outside of the fun and glory of sport. I love seeing strangers hug at bars when their team scores or people bouncing up and down on the bleachers, singing their team to victory. It's important to express emotions as it can be cathartic, and sports games are a safe container to release various emotions we have less of an opportunity to release in our day-to-day lives.

However, I would not want to make important life decisions while watching a close Raider game—or even just before or shortly after—with my rational brain shut down in favor of my emotionally reactive one. I would want to ensure my brain was engaged and I was calm enough to survey information and make an informed decision.

So when it comes to listening to politicians speak, think about why they're saying certain words to you. Is this just theater to stir your emotions? Are they saying something of substance?

When it comes to political theater, it's important to realize when your emotions are being manipulated and how you're being taught to support a political party like a sports team. Politics should not be treated like a game. You're allowed to change your mind, and a special party affiliation need not become a part of your identity in the same way a sports team does. Politics, when it is functioning healthily—and unlike sports—isn't a competitive endeavor about winning and losing. It's about progress, making the country and world better for everyone, and ensuring the interests of the people are at the heart of decision-making.

Making Sense

What does "sense" mean? What does making sense mean? Back to official definitions, this time from the *Cambridge Dictionary*, which defines "making sense" as "clear and easy to understand." The dictionary also uses the word "reasonable," and the definition of reason is "of logical defense."

For my purposes, I want to create my own definition of the phrase "making sense." Something makes sense when it is in harmony with my five senses—sight, smell, hearing, touch, and my personal favorite, taste.

When making important decisions, which include political decisions like voting, I try to leave my emotions behind and ensure to use the harmony of my senses to make the best choices. It's important not to let politicians or media personalities manipulate you into an emotional state of their choosing. They are trying to confuse you and then act like they are the "controlling" answer to that confusion.

Why Would Anyone Want To Be A Politician?

Most do, especially career politicians, because of money (and the power that comes with it). Let's explore a couple of facts.

The US economy is $26 trillion.

The federal budget for 2023 is $5.8 trillion.

Money was not mentioned much in my house growing up. Accumulating as much money as possible was never a goal or a topic of discussion. It is foreign to me how much money rules some people. For some, it's their god. Unfortunately, people with this behavior find politics as a vehicle to accumulate wealth.

Most people would be happy to have the following basics: shelter, warmth, the ability to feed their families, and access to education. Perhaps a vacation or two each year. And there would be enough to go around. The basics without having to work two or three jobs.

Unfortunately, there are people who value money above all else, and it leads to corruption.

There are two books providing a comprehensive reporting of corruption in America. These two books are a blueprint for ending corruption.

In her book *On Corruption in America*, Sarah Chayes does an excellent job discussing the history of money, corruption, and how money has a corrupting influence in society. If you want to know serious facts about corruption in

America, I recommend you read this book. Sarah and her peers are a national treasure. We have scholars like them who spend six to eight years studying to be experts in their field and publishing books so the rest of us can have access to the knowledge they learned over a lifetime, and they should be recognized and appreciated. Do yourself a favor and read or listen to part one, chapter 3, "Aristotle's Views on Money."

Another important book is Jane Mayer's *Dark Money*. In *Dark Money,* Jane Mayer outlines how a person who makes $ 1 billion a year in salary spends $400 million protecting their income. Protecting it by making sure the legislation passed does not interfere with his business. Mayer also demonstrates in great detail how those with a lot of money have created think tanks to spread their message to the American people. The information seems to come from ordinary citizens or neutral academics, but the message is from large corporations that fund these think tanks. This messaging has been going on for decades and is now a part of our collective fabric.

Chapter Two

DIVISION

How Did the Country Get So Divided?

It started in the early 1990s. Congress was held by the Democrats from the 74th Congress (1935-1937) to the 103rd Congress (1993-1995) every year with one exception, the 80th Congress (1945-1947). For fifty-eight years, Democrats controlled Congress.

Republicans could not win the House based on their platform. So Newt Gingrich convinced his fellow Republicans to join him in unfairly discrediting the Democrats. He created the message that not only were Democrats' policies bad for America, but Democrats themselves were evil. He instilled fear into the Republican voters by lying. The messaging worked, the Republicans won the House in 1995, and they have been preaching that same lie for the last thirty years, and that lie—as anything repeated tends to be—has been internalized as truth for many people. This is the origin of our division. And I believe 99 percent of people are not evil, Democrat or Republican. Most of us want to live good lives and ensure we are healthy, happy, and fulfilled. Thinking of our political others as enemies or evil takes away their humanity and easily distorts the truth.

It does not make sense that half of the country, or 80 million, who voted Democrat in the last cycle would want to harm the United States. Take a step back and think about it. I am sure you know Democrats who are good people—and if you know some who are good people, chances are there are many others who are too. The same message goes to Democrats; I'm sure you know Republicans that are good people. I know I do. But it is up to each and every one of us not to let professional politicians divide us. When they do, they win, and they do not care that the country loses as a result.

This division works for candidates to grab power. It works to raise money and get elected, but it does not work for running a country. We are being played by the politicians who try to instill fear by creating a monster of the other side. The monster doesn't exist; we're led to falsely believe in the inhumanity of what or who we perceive as the "other." They are putting forward a false narrative and description. There's a distinction between your fellow citizens who vote for Democrats and Democrats themselves who are politicians. The citizens are fellow Americans like you and me—don't buy into the thirty-year-old lie.

This thirty-year lie instilled distrust in our federal government, and our institutions created the false narrative about a deep state. This concept has no basis in truth.

The result of Gingrich's strategy was to eliminate compromise. The book by Jonathan Rauch, *The Constitution of Knowledge,* states that compromise was one of the pillars of the Constitution. James Madison, who is given credit for writing most of the Constitution, created the forces of the three branches of government so compromise could be used to settle differences. The removal of compromise

28

broke the spirit of the Constitution. That's not very patriotic now, is it?

The only path to improve our institutions is to work with the institutions and Congress. If the voters want to conduct an audit of each federal department, that would be a reasonable request. We have the technology and communication tools to have an open, transparent review of each department. In order for this to work, we need representatives who can work together with the common goal of making our government more efficient and transparent.

The number of years the party had control of Congress:

Democrats 28, Republicans 2

House				
Congress	**Years**	**Total**	**Dems**	**Reps**
73rd	1933-1935	435	313	117
74th	1935-1937	435	322	103
75th	1937-1939	435	333	89

76th	1939-1941	435	262	169
77th	1941-1943	435	267	162
78th	1943-1945	435	222	209
79th	1945-1947	435	243	190
80th	1947-1949	435	188	246
81st	1949-1951	435	263	171
82nd	1951-1953	435	234	199
83rd	1953-1955	435	213	221
84th	1955-1957	435	232	203
85th	1957-1959	435	234	201
86th	1959-1961	435	283	153
87th	1961-1963	435	262	175
88th	1963-1965	435	258	176
89th	1965-1967	435	295	140
90th	1967-1969	435	248	187
91st	1969-1971	435	243	192
92nd	1971-1973	435	255	180
93rd	1973-1975	435	242	192

94th	1975-1977	435	291	144
95th	1977-1979	435	292	143
96th	1979-1981	435	277	158
97th	1981-1983	435	242	192
98th	1983-1985	435	269	166
99th	1985-1987	435	253	182
100th	1987-1989	435	258	177
101st	1989-1991	435	260	175
102nd	1991-1993	435	267	167
103rd	1993-1995	435	258	176
104th	1995-1997	435	204	230

The Trump Brand

Trump deserves a lot of credit for putting the coalition together. I recommend we continue referring to the coalition as Trump's coalition. I know Trump is excellent at driving our emotions. He has something highly intelligent about him, given he knows how to manipulate a television audience—he was a reality television star, after all. I think we can continue to use Trump's brand, but it's time we look for a new leader who has better principles, wants to better the country, and is more committed to truth-seeking and truth-telling. The Trump coalition deserves better than Trump. Remember that he's meant to work for you. All political leaders do. Consider moving your support to a new leader who will listen to your rational and pragmatic needs.

Truth

Is it asking too much for our leaders to be truthful? My concern is if lying is accepted by our leaders, then it trickles down to our businesses, communities, and families. Eventually, you'll find your son, daughter, or spouse lying to be the norm. We must not normalize lying.

Trump was taught to lie by his father. He learned to use lying as a technique when negotiating, as it was all about winning—ethics were barely an afterthought. It is foreign to me to lie so deeply to gain an upper hand over someone—to make promises you cannot keep. If you don't understand or agree that Trump lies constantly, I recommend you look more deeply into the issue. The evidence is overwhelming. Until the Trump Coalition comes to terms with the truth about Trump's lying, we are a weak coalition, and the potential for change will be wasted.

In *The Death of Truth*, Michiko Kakutani wrote about the history of lying and how political leaders use it to gain power. He stated Trump's first lie as president was the numbers in attendance at his inauguration. He said one and a half million people were there when, in fact, it was 250,000. Trump told this lie as preparation to lie on a regular basis, letting us know there was nothing we could do about it. He was preparing us for a constant stream of lies so we would be conditioned for the big lie that the election was fraudulent.

In a podcast with Sam Harris and the historian Yuval Noah Harari, Harari said, "Without trust, all civilizations collapse." Is there anything more serious?

Harari then provided some details that the worldwide monetary system would collapse. The whole concept of money is based on trust. For the monetary system to function properly, there needs to be trust.

What is the relationship between trust and truth? I had to go back to my dictionary. Truth is what precedes trust. Without truth, there cannot be trust. Without trust, things collapse.

Do you see how important truth-telling is? We cannot clean up Washington and accept lying as normal. Lying is not normal. We each must persevere and seek the truth.

January 6th

When I think of the storming of The Capitol on January 6th, I think of the nine people who died. They are Kevin Greeson, Benjamin Phillips, Rosanne Boyland, Ashli Babbitt, Brian Sicknick, Howard Liebengood, Jeffrey Smith, Gunther Hashida, and Kyle DeFreytag.

I think of the hundreds of people who lost their jobs for participating in the event. I think about those in prison or jail right now because they made an emotional decision based on a lie.

One example is Richard Barnett, who had a photo of himself with his feet propped up on Nancy Pelosi's desk. His attorney described Barnett as "this crazy redneck from Arkansas," given to "hootin' and hollerin'," who "got pushed into The Capitol and put his feet up on the wrong person's desk."

He cast Barnett as a harmless windbag — "that nutty uncle" who has "no sense of boundaries" or "societal norms," who "doesn't necessarily fit in today's world" and "routinely offends others" with political incorrectness. Barnett, with a wry smile, admitted he is "sometimes a loudmouth." He also is a "loving father and husband," he told the jury, and an ardent "patriot." Trump has a pattern of exploiting the most vulnerable and exploiting their trust for campaign donations or to fight the fights he starts.

Richard Barnett was sentenced to 4.5 years in prison. Although his crime pertained to what he did on January 6th, it all started with trusting Donald Trump. As that trust was broken, his freedom "collapsed." Trump didn't care about Barnett or the other people in the Capitol. Trump cared about overturning the election and "winning" it to satisfy his ego. He didn't care who lost along the way, his supporters included, as long as he won.

This could have been you or your son or daughter or husband. Maybe you had a friend or relative in Washington on January 6th. If so, especially if it affected your life profoundly, please email me your story (address provided at the end of this book).

Trump took no risk on January 6th. If it succeeded, he would be president. If it failed, his supporters would go to jail. This is like playing poker with other people's money, but Trump gambled with other people's lives instead of money.

Betrayal

Trump is labeled a "populist," which means a person, especially a politician, who strives to appeal to ordinary people who feel their concerns are disregarded by established elite groups. Trump showed little regard for his followers on January 6th. He betrayed them. And it could have been a lot worse if it wasn't for the restraint shown by The Capitol police.

He showed his true colors that he was an elitist, not a populist. He didn't care who went down in his quest to "win-at-all-costs." Remember above how we talked about what people would do to accumulate more money? Trump suffers from this affliction. His desire to be in charge of the United States's money was more important to him than the lives of the people in the crowd who he sent to the Capitol.

Remember how Trump promised to drain the swamp? He didn't get close to that pledge. In fact, he was yet another opportunistic "gator" swimming in its waters.

For starters, Trump's tweet about Mike Pence was reckless. Eleven minutes after the Capitol was stormed, he tweeted that Pence "didn't have the courage to do what should have been done to protect our Country and our Constitution." Trump put his desire for money over Mike Pence's life.

On January 6th, Trump knew there was no voter fraud. He was told by his Department of Justice, Bill Barr, in early December and Christopher Krebs, whose team from Homeland Security was responsible for preparing our election system for the election.

As of January 6th, Trump's legal team had filed 60 lawsuits in dozens of state and federal courts claiming irregularities and fraud. The legal team failed to submit any evidence or facts and lost all 60 lawsuits. 0-60. The numbers don't look good.

Today, in the summer of 2023, no one who has studied this subject and is honest with themselves believes the election was stolen. Sadly, we have many elected officials and media personalities who repeat this lie because it makes them money to do so. If you still believe the election was stolen, you are a victim of what happens when a lie is repeated over and over. The election was not stolen. If you want to make America great, it starts with understanding the 2020 election was legitimate.

January 6th was premeditated and highly promoted by Trump and his lieutenants like Steve Bannon. Trump also knew people in the crowd carried weapons. Yet he told them to go "fight like hell"—a clear call to arms and to utilize violence. Trump put many lives, and the American system itself, in danger. I believe Trump should be charged with manslaughter for the nine people who died. He has not been charged, proving we have a two-tier system in America where the elite and political class are protected. Another reason is the Department of Justice (DOJ) is concerned about how you, the Trump supporter, will react. The Republican party leaders will say these charges are politically motivated. The truth is Trump premeditated the rally months in advance, then promoted it as a violent protest; the people who attended were armed, and he sent them to The Capitol to "fight like hell.". We must support the DOJ's efforts to enforce the rule of law.

With Trump endeavoring to run for office again, it is imperative we find a better leader. Trump betrayed his most loyal supporters. He doesn't truly care about you; he cares about money and power. He just uses you for political gain. Trump served his purpose by putting the coalition together. It is now time for the coalition to use its power to enable change in Washington.

Fox News, the Dominion Lawsuit, and Tucker Carlson's Comments

As a result of the Dominion lawsuit—a lawsuit against Fox News which will determine if they are financially liable for spreading the falsehood the 2020 election was rigged by voting machines—news anchor Tucker Carlson's text messages have been made public. These messages confirm three important truths.

The first is that Fox News knew the election was *not* stolen, the second is they tried to cover up the fact Trump fairly lost the election, and the third is that Tucker Carlson did not care for Trump and only pretended to support him to increase Fox News' ratings. Here are the messages as reported by Josh Marcus in the *Independent* on March 8, 2023: "We are very, very close to being able to ignore Trump most nights," Carlson told an unknown Fox News employee just two days before the January 6th Capitol riot, according to the court documents. "I truly can't wait."

"I hate him passionately," he added.

In other disclosures, Carlson called Mr. Trump "a demonic force, a destroyer," while labeling Mr. Trump's campaign officials and attorneys as liars spreading "offensive" conspiracies about the election.

"It's unbelievably offensive to me," Carlson said in one exchange. "Our viewers are good people, and they believe it."

Carlson isn't the only one mentioned in the newly released court documents.

Rupert Murdoch, the media mogul who owns the network, was captured elsewhere wondering if Fox News hosts like Sean Hannity and Laura Ingraham had gone "too far" with their election coverage.

"I would have liked us to be stronger in denouncing it in hindsight," Murdoch said during a deposition, according to court documents.

In another *Independent* article by Joe Sommerlad, published on Tuesday, April 25, 2023, he captured this quote from Carlson showing clearly Fox News wanted to report the outcome of the election falsely: In another message purportedly sent to a group chat including Ingraham and Hannity on November 12, a week after the US had gone to the polls, Carlson pointed out a tweet from the network's White House correspondent, Jacqui Heinrich, in which she fact-checked a post by Mr. Trump alleging voter fraud.

In it, she pointed out that "top election infrastructure officials" had declared "there is no evidence that any voting system deleted or lost votes, changed votes or was in any way compromised."

Carlson reacted by saying: "Please get her fired. Seriously . . . What the f***? I'm actually shocked. . . . It needs to stop tonight immediately, like tonight. It's immeasurably hurting the company. The stock price is down. Not a joke."

Given his comments elsewhere, this appears to be a demonstration of loyalty toward the carefully cultivated Fox brand and not an attempt to shield Mr. Trump from criticism.

What we learned from the above text message exchange from Tucker Carlson to his colleagues and from Murdoch's statement is that Fox News understood the election was not rigged—they decided to convey a different message on air in front of rolling cameras to their audience to protect their ratings. We also learned that despite years of showing support for Trump, Carlson doesn't care for him at all. What we should learn from the above evidence made public by the Dominion case is that Trump, Fox News, and Tucker Carlson can not be trusted as sources of truthful information.

The Indictment for Mishandling Classified Documents

In 2023, Trump was indicted for his mishandling of classified documents. As of the time of writing, this is a still-unfolding development. Mitt Romney said, "Trump brought these charges upon himself by not only taking the classified documents but by refusing to simply return them when given numerous opportunities to do so." Reading Mitt Romney's statement and the statements of others, I would word it differently. The DOJ begged Trump informally and formally with a subpoena to return the documents, and Trump refused. Trump dared the DOJ to file charges and left the DOJ no choice.

But all is not lost. Let's look at the possible Republican candidates for 2024 and think about who might be best to go forward.

Chapter Three

SOLUTION

To solve the issue, we need to find a Republican candidate who would be a far better fit than Trump. Let's look at people who are vying for the presidency and whether they might be good or bad for the country.

Florida Governor Ron DeSantis disqualified himself when, as a political stunt, he flew migrants from Florida to Massachusetts. It appears he did this to make a point of sending migrants from a Republican-majority state to a Democrat-majority state. He tricked the migrants and played with human lives for political gain. What sort of man could be so deceitful to fellow humans? It does not take a religious scholar to see how wrong this is.

In all my years of reading history, I've never read of a time when a hateful leader has done good. If we want to shift the norm from today's constant political arguing to civil discourse, we need to elect someone civil.

I think to find a new leader. We need to look outside of Trump's orbit and beyond the current list of candidates. The one that leaps out most to me is Adam Kinzinger. He is forty-five and could serve two terms. He joined the Air Force in 2003 and is currently a lieutenant colonel in the Air National Guard. Adam served as the United States representative for Illinois from 2011 to 2023. I like that he's not running because it shows he isn't just power-hungry. That means we need to recruit him. I don't trust *anyone* who volunteers to run for president.

Adam demonstrated with the January 6th hearings he is principled by breaking with the Republican leadership to form part of the January 6th Committee to uncover the facts of what happened. He has character. He would listen to the pragmatic ideas of the Trump Coalition. He would implement the changes you want in relation to the twenty-four-year plan we'll discuss shortly.

If we cannot convince Adam Kinzinger to join the race, there are a few other candidates already running who have good reputations and are a better choice for the GOP nomination who would run on a populist platform. They are, in no particular order, Asa Hutchinson, Nikki Haley, Tim Scott, and Chris Christie. To keep the coalition together and make it clear who has the power, I would recommend promoting the new leader as follows: Trump Coalition for Asa or Trump Coalition for Nikki, etc. Go out and start making your signs.

If you want to witness your power in action, send $10 to any of these candidates and see how fast the national conversation changes. The candidate who receives your donation will understand it comes from the grassroots level and not be beholden to large money or corporations. They will be beholden to us, the people.

The other candidates running for the GOP nomination are not populists. At best, they are representatives of big money; at worst, they are yet another power-hungry conman.

The Real Populist Movement

As we try to identify candidates and organizations that we can trust, It's a good time to discuss the big surprise of the 2020 election. It happened on the Democrat side of the race. The biggest surprise by far was the success of Andrew Yang. The DNC (Democratic National Committee) went to great effort to have Yang withdraw from the race. The DNC changed the criteria for debate qualification by increasing fundraising goals and poll results. Surprisingly, Yang met the new requirements and was on every debate stage. Yang's success was due to his honest, accurate assessment of today's political environment and his pragmatic solutions to solve the country's problems. Yang is a real populist in today's politics. He has started a new political organization called the Forward Party to compete with the established two parties. If you are looking for a source of fact-based information and clear thinking with new ideas, I recommend checking it out.

So Who Is the Bad Guy?

If we need a bad guy—and I am learning it's easier if we have one—we should conclude the number one bad guy is money. The money it takes to run for Congress or Senate is beyond the reach of an ordinary citizen.

The results are those with a large amount of wealth, including corporations, have a disproportionate say in who gets elected and what legislation gets passed. The good news is we outnumber them, but we have to vote together.

Chapter Four

OUR 24-YEAR-PLAN. OUR NORTH STAR.

Let's create a twenty-four-year plan for the country. Imagine what you would want life to be like in 2048, and let's create a plan to achieve this vision.

This should eliminate some of the unprofessional behavior in Washington, truly drain the swamp, and set our country on course for prosperity and success.

I will present my ideas just as they are—ideas. I am open to your thoughts and feedback. You can email your vision of America in 2048 to the email I've provided at the end of this book. This is your chance to be heard.

So far, we have these priorities:

1. Finishing the job of draining the swamp by passing the proposed Election Integrity amendment.

2. The government is to ensure the American people are getting their fair share of the economic pie.

3. Establish an energy plan. One for the next ten years (short term) and a second 24-year-plan (long term). The ten-year plan should look at domestic energy sources. The long-term plan needs to include reviving our Nuclear Power industry.

4. Develop a 24-year plan to reduce the national debt.

5. Fix social media so it's safe for our children and society.

Earlier, we explored how the US economy is $26 trillion dollars. About 70 percent of this is because Americans are spending their money. This means consumers are spending 70 percent of our economy, which equates to $18 trillion. What would the huge corporations do without you as the consumer? They wouldn't exist. Apple, Microsoft, Facebook, Amazon, Visa, Netflix, Disney, Wal-Mart, Exxon, etc. The total value of these companies is over $6 trillion. But they are only of this value because you, the consumer, spend your money on them.

We learned earlier there is too much greed at the executive level of our large corporations and some politicians. I would argue there is too little greed among the average citizen. I want you to vote for candidates that will improve your economic situation. I have yet to hear from any candidate how they will put more money in your pocket, which will help you feed your family, afford your house, and go on vacation occasionally.

A survey conducted by Bankrate found that 56 percent of Americans could not afford an unexpected $1,000 expense. *Reuters* reported on March 9, 2023, that household wealth is $147 trillion. That means 40 percent of the country has $147 trillion in savings, and 60 percent has zero.

Let me summarize. The United States' economy is based on American citizens buying products and services. This consumption is generating $18 trillion in gross national product. It is also creating the value of our leading corporation. S&P 500 Market Cap is currently $34.34 trillion, but 60 percent of the country does not have disposable income.

Education

Pre K -12

We should demand the best education for our children. The National Children's Book Literacy Alliance states only 35 percent of fourth graders are reading at or above grade level.

We should leverage working programs. Tennessee has had success with its reading program. The department's Reading 360 initiative and other supports have created a comprehensive approach to ensure Tennessee can boost reading skills in kindergarten through third grade to students who can already read at grade level.

Let's set some goals for our eighth graders. Since I am located in Silicon Valley, my ideas are often tech-oriented. I would welcome your ideas for a class project for eighth graders. My idea is to have each eighth-grade class develop and publish an app so they can keep up with the times.

We are not taking advantage of the internet to help with education. What is the future of learning? How do we make it accessible to everyone? Is John Green's Crash Course being promoted widely? Should we use more sites like Khan Academy?

The solution for upward mobility is education. We need to do a better job of using today's technology to educate more people. On the Secretary of Education's website, we should provide as many resources as possible to help educate our populace.

We need a national discussion, accessible on the web, about education. Identify the best practices and aggressively promote them.

College

The biggest form of discrimination is not black vs. white or gay vs. straight. It is college-educated vs. non-college-educated.

We need to implement programs to increase the college graduation rate from the low thirties to 60 percent. In Taiwan, the college graduation rate is 80 percent. That means a high number of their population is educated, and education often directly correlates to income.

Another problem colleges could solve is integrating and mixing young adults from different regions. College could also be an opportunity for our young adults to move to another part of the country. Instead of charging more for out-of-state tuition, maybe we should explore the benefits of using college to mix up our population.

We should take advantage of the internet to reduce the cost of a four-year degree. I went to a community college before transferring to a university. By the time I transferred, I was twenty-one years old, much more mature than I was at eighteen. The cost of my first two years was only a few hundred dollars.

Since our military receives a big portion of our federal budget, can they implement a program to provide bachelor's degrees to the enlisted men they recognize as having the potential?

Re-Building our Cities and Creating Local News

We need to invest in small cities across the country. The country would not serve well if only the East and West Coast have all of the high-paying jobs. As part of rebuilding our cities, we need to provide funding for local newspapers/news outlets. The idea is local news is more likely to be trusted and has the ability to keep the local officials honest. The only criterion to work at a local newspaper is the person needs to be from the town or city.

While I Have You, I Have One Last Item.

In 2000 Robert Putnam published the book *Bowling Alone.* In it, Putnam explained the collapse of the community and the growing problem of isolation and loneliness in America. On May 6, 2023, the US Surgeon General Dr. Vivek Murthy published a report declaring loneliness a new public health epidemic in the United States. It stated, "Our epidemic of loneliness and isolation has been an underappreciated public health crisis that has harmed individuals and societal health."

This is a problem we can solve. If you have the ability, invite your neighbor, old high school friend, or work colleague for coffee, a beer, a hike, a BBQ, etc. A few times a year or a few times over multiple years would make all the difference.

Conclusion

Your vote and your $10 donation are the source of power in Washington. You move your vote, and your donation, and the power moves with it. You are kind, morally sound, and want the best for the country. Trump doesn't possess any of those qualities. Adam Kinzinger does. So do Tim Scott, Asa Hutchinson, Nikki Haley, and Chris Christie.

You have a seat at the table, and the legislation you propose can be implemented as long as it is rational and pragmatic. I look forward to learning about your proposed legislation.

We, as a people, have so much unfinished business to complete. It's up to us to end the divide in this country so we can move forward. If twenty million Trump voters embraced working for the good of the country—regardless of political party—the national discourse would change overnight. Let's start supporting alternative candidates now so we can have as many candidates as possible to participate in the debates.

You have a great responsibility, and I believe in you to make a decision supporting a candidate who is ethical, has deep values, and helps get the United States of America to the place it deserves to be. Let's make this country the place of prosperity, love, and kindness. Not just for ourselves but also for the lives, and the future, of our children.

Sources of Information Demonstrating Safety from Misinformation

Fareed Zakaria Global Public Square (GPS) Podcast: Fareed has provided a balanced and fair summary of current events for fifteen years. You don't need a lot of information. You need quality, and Fareed is quality.

Freakonomics: This is a non-political podcast with general knowledge based on facts and science.

The Guardian: British publication left of center.

The Economist: British publication moderate and independent of any special interest.

The Forward Party and Andrew Yang

Country First and Adam Kinzinger

Sources of Information Demonstrating the Promotion of Hate Speech and Misinformation

Fox News

Tucker Carlson

Steve Bannon

My Contact Information:
Kevin@Themiddleusa.org